BLACK LEGACY PRESS™
WWW.BLACKLEGACYPRESS.ORG

NEGRO JOURNALISM

BY
GEORGE W. GORE, JR.

BLP PUBLISHING
Eastchester New York

For wholesale please visit:
www.BBWLogistics.com

Available wherever books are sold.

ISBN: 978-1-63652-152-7

NEGRO JOURNALISM

An Essay on the History and Present
Conditions of the Negro Press

by

GEORGE W. GORE, JR.

PREFACE

This pamphlet does not pretend to be a detailed or scholarly discussion of the subject. Lack of experience and funds have limited the author to a mere outlining or suggesting of the field. In fact, this essay is only the expansion of a term paper submitted in fulfillment of a semester requirement in the Course in Journalism.

The main purpose of this essay is to show the various stages of development through which the Negro press has evolved with a view of furnishing a background for the better understanding of its present status. It is written, too, to present the problems and inherent possibilities of Negro Journalism; to point out the progress which is being made today; and to suggest future possibilities. If this attempt, amateur and incomplete as it may be, in any measure awakens an interest in the achievements and efforts of Negro newspapers and magazines it has served its purpose.

For the period up to 1890, the author frequently has referred to *The Afro-American* Press and Its Editors by I. Garland Penn—a work which is an authority on the subject for the period covered by it. A large part of the biographical data and information on present day newspapers was obtained from the Negro Year Book and communications. I especially wish to thank those editors and publishers who so kindly gave me the information which I desired.

I am also very grateful to The Chicago Defender and The Southern Workman of Hampton, Va., for the loan of some cuts.

Especially do I wish to acknowledge the valuable assistance and helpful criticism of my instructor, Prof. L. E. Mitchell, director of the Course in Journalism, in DePauw University.

GEORGE W. GORE, JR.

Greencastle, Indiana.

CONTENTS

Chapter IX
Training In Negro Schools 35

Chapter X
A Forecast Of The Future...39

CHAPTER I

EARLY NEGRO NEWSPAPERS

FREEDOM'S JOURNAL

Seven years after Benjamin Lundy began *The Genius of Universal Emancipation*, and four years before William Lloyd Garrison started to publish *The Liberator*, Negro Journalism in America was born. The first publication was *Freedom's Journal*, issued March 16, 1827. It was in form a medium-sized, neat-looking, well-printed weekly, about nine by twelve inches. *Freedom's Journal* was a thorough-going abolitionist sheet, having been called into being to defend the Negro against the vile attacks of a New York editor of Jewish descent who had pro-slavery and Negro-hating tendencies. This new organ had for its motto, "Righteousness Exalteth a Nation," and its columns were filled with long dissertations on the immorality of slavery.

JOHN RUSSWURM FIRST EDITOR

The editor, John Russwurm, one of the first Negroes to graduate from a college in the United States, graduated from Bowdoin College in 1826. Russwurm was born in Jamaica in 1799. He published *The Journal* until 1829, when he went to Liberia, where he became editor of *The Liberia Herald*.

THE COLORED AMERICAN

A period of about eight years elapsed before the founding of a second Negro newspaper. In January, 1837,

Rev. Samuel Cornish began the publishing of *The Weekly Advocate*. The name was changed in March, however, to *The Colored American*, and under that name it continued to be issued weekly until 1842. The first editor, Rev. Cornish, was one of the leading Negro journalists of the period. He had been associated with *Freedom's Journal*, and throughout a period of twenty years he was actively connected with some newspaper.

Advocated Emancipation

The subscription price of *The Colored American* was two dollars per year in advance. Its objects were, according to its flag, "the moral, social and political elevation of the free Colored people; and the peaceful emancipation of the enslaved." The paper was well received by the American press of the period, and many favorable comments on it appeared from time to time.

The Elevator

The first two Negro newspapers had their headquarters in New York City, but their successor was established in Albany, N. Y. *The Elevator* came into being in 1842, with Stephen Myers as its publisher. The paper was strongly backed by the Abolitionists. Among its influential supporters and backers was Horace Greeley of *The New York Tribune*.

The National Watchman

Contemporaneous with *The Elevator* appeared *The National Watchman and Clarion*, which was established in Troy, N. Y., in the latter part of 1842. Its publisher and editor was William G. Allen. It was short-lived, as was also *The People's Press* which was published by Thomas Hamilton in New York City the following year.

THE MYSTERY

Following the lead taken by the empire state, Pennsylvania became a field of activity for the Negro journalist. In 1843, *The Mystery* was published at Pittsburgh by Dr. Martin Delaney, a graduate of Harvard College. At first it was conducted as the personal property of its editor, but as such it survived only nine months when it became necessary to transfer its ownership to a joint-stock company. After the change Delaney was retained in the capacity of editor.

Delaney was the first Negro editor to be sued for libel. He was fined for his statements; but his popularity was so great that the fine was paid by popular subscription.

The Mystery ceased publication under that name in 1848, at which time it was purchased by the African Methodist Episcopal Church.

STATEMENT BY N. Y. SUN, ORIGIN OF THE RAM'S HORN

As the result of a statement by the editor of *The New York Sun*, "The *Sun* shines for all white men and not for colored men," in January, 1847, *The Ram's Horn* was begun. Its editor was Willis Hodges, who according to *The Afro-American Press and Its Editor*, furnished the money necessary to publish the first issue by whitewashing in New York City for two months. Within a short period of time the circulation of the paper reached two thousand five hundred copies. The subscription price was $1.50 to subscribers within the state, and $1 a year to those outside the state. Its motto was—"We are men, and therefore interested in whatever concerns men." The publication was a five column folio, printed on both sides. It suspended publication in June 1848.

[1]March 21, 1828, the name was changed to *Rights of All*.

[2]Published by I. Garland Penn in 1891.

CHAPTER II
THE ABOLITIONIST PRESS (1847-1865)

DOUGLASS FOUNDS NORTH STAR

With the founding of the *North Star*, at Rochester. N. Y., November 1, 1847, a new era in Negro Journalism was begun. The new paper was conducted on a much higher plane than any of the preceding publications. The editor of the *North Star* was Frederick Douglass, a man who stood head and shoulders above his colleagues. In fact, Douglass is in Negro Journalism what Bennett, or Pulitzer, or Greeley, or Dana is in American Journalism. The personal fame of the man gave his paper at once a place among the first journals of the country.

The columns of the *North Star* were filled with contributions from correspondents in Europe and the West Indies, as well as from all parts of the United States. It was the first Negro newspaper to have any considerable circulation among the American people outside of its own race group.

LIFE OF FRED DOUGLASS

The life of the founder of this paper is a most interesting one. Born a slave at Tuckahoe, Md., February, 1817, he escaped from his master in 1833, going first to New York City, and then to New Bedford, Mass. In 1841, he was sent out as a lecturer under the auspices of the Massachusetts Anti-Slavery Society. He was one of the most prominent anti-slavery agitators of his day; a series of lectures on the immorality of human slavery was given by him in England. Douglass' power as a writer was great, and his ready and vigorous use of the English language was always effective. The paper was discontinued shortly after the abolition of slavery.

THE IMPARTIAL CITIZEN

Around the brilliancy of the *North Star* moved several satellites, which somewhat reflected the light of the major planet. Among these was *The Impartial Citizen*, published at Syracuse, N. Y., in 1848, by Samuel Ward. It is said that the paper was conducted on a high plane and was ably edited.

COLORED MAN'S JOURNAL RUNS TEN YEARS

The suspension of *The Ram's Horn* in 1848 left the Negroes of New York City without a newspaper. However, in 1851, Louis H. Putman began the publication of *The Colored Man's Journal*. It was backed by a friend who financially supported it, and as a result the paper was able to run for a period of ten years—a record unequalled during the period before the Emancipation by any paper with the exception of the *North Star*.

ALIENATED AMERICAN

The Alienated American, edited by W. H. Day, was the first Negro newspaper published in Ohio. It entered upon its career in Cleveland, Ohio, in 1852, five years after its editor was graduated from Oberlin College. *The Alienated American* was one of the best journals published by Negroes in the nineteenth century.

Day was a prolific, scholarly writer. His publication was a creditable one and realized a good support. The paper ceased publication in 1856, when its editor made a trip to England.

A. M. E. Church Buys The Mystery

In 1848, the African Methodist Episcopal Church purchased *The Mystery* of Pittsburgh, Pa., of which Martin Delaney was editor. During the four years of its existence in Pittsburgh, the paper was known as the *Christian Herald*. In 1852, the paper was moved to Philadelphia, and its name was changed to *Christian Recorder*. Rev, M. M. Clarke became its first editor.

Christian Recorder Oldest Negro Newspaper

The beginning of the *Christian Recorder* in 1852, marks the founding of the oldest Negro newspaper in existence today. It is also significant in that it marks the first serious attempt in Negro Journalism to establish a religious newspaper. The early years of the paper were beset with many difficulties, and oftimes the paper was not issued regularly. Not until Elisha Weaver became editor in 1861 did it appear weekly. The size of the paper has increased from 5 columns, 4 pages, 12 by 16 inches, in 1848, to its present size, 4 columns, 16 pages, 10 by 16 inches.

The present circulation of the paper is about 5,000. Its editor is R. R. Wright Jr., who received the degree of Ph.D. from the University of Pennsylvania in 1911.

Negro Journalism on Pacific Coast

The year 1855 saw Negro Journalism starting on the Pacific coast. Within a space of less than thirty years Negro Journalism had made its way from the Atlantic to the Pacific seaboard. The first publication was established at San Francisco under the name of *The Mirror of the Times*. Its editor was Judge Gibbs. It was published for seven years, and in 1862 was merged into *The Pacific Appeal*.

THE HERALD OF FREEDOM

Another contemporary of the *North Star* was *The Herald of Freedom*, published in 1855, in Ohio, by Peter H. Clark. It was short-lived but during its existence it was one of the best advocates of Abolition. Its editor was a man of good common sense and vast knowledge. After the suspension of his paper, Clark was associated with Douglass on the *North Star*.

THE ANGLO-AFRICAN

Thomas Hamilton, the publisher of the short-lived *People's Press*, again attempted a publication in New York City. On July 23, 1859, he began publishing *The Anglo-African*. The paper was well printed and in the opinion of Frederick Douglass "had more promise and more journalistic ability about it, than any of the other papers." The motto of the papers of the period was highly indicative of their editorial outlook and policy. Practically every paper had its motto, and *The Anglo-African* was no exception. Its motto was: "Man must be free; if not through law, then above the law."

ADVOCATES HAYTIAN EMIGRATION

In 1860, the paper was bought by James Redpath—the object of his purchase being to advocate the Haytian Emigration Movement. With the change in ownership the paper was known as *The Weekly Anglo-African*. Later, in 1861, the paper reverted to the Hamilton family, being published by Robert Hamilton. The original name of the paper was resumed, and under its new publisher became an ardent supporter of the Republican party. With the freeing of the slaves, *The Anglo-African* began to advocate the need of educational facilities for the freedman, especially in the South. The paper was suspended shortly after Emancipation.

Colored Citizen Organ of Negro Soldiers During War

During the period of the Civil War only two Negro newspapers were established, one of which was *The Colored Citizen*, published at Cincinnati, Ohio, by John P. Sampson. It was issued in the interest of the Negro soldiers fighting in the war. It was commonly referred to as the "Soldiers' Organ," and was widely disseminated among the soldiers. Sampson was well educated—being a product of the Boston public school system—and as an editor he was both able and enterprising. *The Colored Citizen* was suspended the latter part of 1865.

The Pacific Appeal

In 1862, *The Pacific Appeal* came into being in San Francisco, but it was not a new publication, however, it was merely the successor to *The Mirror of the Times*. Its editor was William H. Carter. It became the index of the activities of the Negroes on the Pacific coast. The paper's motto was: "He who would be free, himself must strike the blow." It was a six column folio, well-printed, and contained editorials which on the whole were sober and sound.

The Elevator, Edited by Bell

The second paper established on the western coast was *The Elevator*, which was begun by Phillip Bell, April 18, 1865, in San Francisco, Cal. The paper stated its mission thus: "We shall labor for the civil and political enfranchisement of the Colored people—not as a distinct and separate race, but as American citizens." The publisher encouraged advertisements and quoted his rates as being 60 cents for one insertion and 25 cents for each subsequent insertion.

Bell a Man of Learning

Bell had been connected with the journalistic field for twenty-five years, and as a result was experienced in the work. His editorials were of a high quality. His paper was neatly printed and contained contributions relating to science, art, literature and drama. In fact, it is said that Bell himself was well-versed in belles-lettres and dramatic criticism. By many of his contemporaries he was considered the Napoleon of the Negro press. Although he died in 1889, his paper continued for many years thereafter.

CHAPTER III

THE RECONSTRUCTION PERIOD (1865-1880)

EMANCIPATION GOAL OF NEGRO PRESS

With the emancipation, a new period in Negro Journalism is begun. For nearly forty years newspapers had been published by Negroes who had obtained their freedom, but the circulation of these papers among the race group of necessity was limited. Emancipation marked the realization of the goal of the Negro press prior to that time, and with the ushering in of freedom many of the newspapers ceased publication. There was, however, still another great, if not even more important task for the Negro press—the education of the masses of illiterate. This task the surviving newspapers, together with many new ones, set out to accomplish.

FIRST SOUTHERN NEGRO NEWSPAPER

The first notable development of the period was the beginning of Negro newspapers in the South, where the large majority of Negroes were located. The first Negro newspaper published in the South was *The Colored American* of Augusta, Ga., issued for the first time in October, 1865. The following paragraph from its prospectus will suffice to show the paper's attitude and policy:

COLORED AMERICAN'S PROSPECTUS

"It (*The Colored American*) is designated to be a vehicle for the diffusion of Religious, Political and General Intelligence. It will be devoted to the promotion of harmony and good-will between the whites and Colored people of the south, and untiring in its advocacy of Industry and Education among all classes; but particularly the class most in need of our agency.

"Accepting, at all times, the decision of public sentiment and Legislative Assemblies, and bowing to the majesty of law, it will fearlessly remonstrate against legal and constitutional proscription by appeal to the public sense of justice."

SHUFTEN'S EDITORIAL ON THE RACE PROBLEM

The editor of the paper was J. T. Shuften, who was ably assisted by Dr. James Lynch. Shuften was credited by *The New York World* as having written the best article of the time on the "Negro Question." The paper was short-lived and suspended February, 1866.

PRECURSORS IN SOUTHERN STATES

With the beginning of Negro Journalism in the South, papers sprung up in other states: *The Colored Tennessean* and *The True Communicator*, of Baltimore, Md., being among the more noted ones. Many of the papers were short-lived; others changed hands and names frequently and continued for several years.

PAPERS GROW IN INFLUENCE AND CIRCULATION

The year 1868 saw the founding of *The Charleston Leader*, at Charleston, S. C. By 1870, the Negro press began to make itself felt. *The People's Journal*, with a circulation of over 10,000 was being edited by Dr. R. L. Perry. In Mississippi, James J. Spellman and John Lynch began *The Colored Citizen*. December, 1870, marked the founding of *The New Orleans Louisianian*, by P. B.

S. Pinchback, who in 1873 became governor of Louisiana, being the only Negro ever to hold this position.

Editors Highly Educated

August 1861, John J. Freeman started *The Progressive American*, in New York City, which existed for ten years. The one outstanding achievement of this paper is the fact that as a result of its fight for Negro teachers in the public schools twenty-three were appointed. Between 1865 and 1880, over 30 newspapers of more or less merit came into existence; Negro newspapers were being published in 21 states. The papers of the period were ably edited and were the product of some of the most highly educated Negroes.

[3]Pinchback died in Washington, D. C., Dec. 22, 1921.

[4]Afro-American Press.

CHAPTER IV

THE PERIOD OF TRANSITION (1880-1900)

NUMBER OF PAPERS INCREASES

The last twenty years of the nineteenth century were marked by an increase in the number of papers published. More than 150 papers were being published by Negroes in thirty different states before the dawn of the new century. To trace the history of all of these papers would be useless, if not well nigh impossible, as but few of them were long-lived or permanent. Most of them were started for the achievement of a single end, and having served the temporary need disappeared. There are, however, several papers which were established during this period that demand treatment because of their longevity and present existence.

PHILADELPHIA TRIBUNE

Among this group is *The Philadelphia Tribune*, founded by Christopher J. Perry in 1884. Perry, who was sole owner of his paper, had had much experience in Journalism before becoming a publisher. His work as editor of the Colored Department of *The Sunday Mercury*, had established his reputation as a journalist.

REMARKABLE SUCCESS UNDER PERRY

Since its founding, its editor has worked unceasingly towards its development and as a result the success of the paper has been remarkable. Today the paper exists, and in spite of the death of its founder in 1920, is still carried on by his heirs. Today *The Philadelphia Tribune* occupies an enviable position among Negro papers, and is undoubtedly one of the twelve best Negro papers in the United States. At the time of his death, Christopher Perry was president of The National Negro Press Association.

THE AGE OLDEST NEGRO PAPER IN NEW YORK CITY

The oldest Negro newspaper published in New York City at the present time is *The New York Age*. It was founded in 1888 by T. Thomas Fortune, the living dean of Negro newspaper editors. Fortune began his journalistic career as a boy in the office of a white paper published in Marianna, Fla. His first editorship came in 1880, when he became connected with *The New York Globe*. Under the guidance of Fortune, *The Age* was perhaps the greatest Negro newspaper of the period. Garland Penn, in his *Afro-American Press* (published in 1891), styles, Fortune as "the most noted man in Afro-American journalism."

RICHMOND PLANET EDITED BY MITCHELL

The Richmond Planet, founded by John Mitchell, Jr., in 1884, is another Negro newspaper that has enjoyed longevity. Mitchell seems to have been a born newspaperman, and practically all of his life he has devoted himself to journalism. Despite his location in the Southland, Mitchell has ever been a bold and fearless writer. Today *The Richmond Planet* still exists, with John Mitchell, Jr., at its head, and has a circulation of over 25,000.

SMITH AND THE CLEVELAND GAZETTE

The Cleveland Gazette was begun in August, 1883, with H. C. Smith as sole owner. It was considered as one of the best edited papers in the United States. Smith was an ardent politician, and his editorials advocating Republicanism were exceptionally pointed and well put. The paper was one of the few Negro papers of the period that was a financial success. *The Cleveland Gazette* is still published by H. C. Smith. It has a circulation of approximately 20,000.

WILLIAM CHASE AND THE BEE

Perhaps the strongest Negro newspaper ever published in Washington, D. C., is *The Washington Bee*, of which William Calvin Chase is editor and founder. Chase is especially noted for his bull-dog tenacity in exposing and attacking fraud. He has always been one of the "big guns" in editorial artillery. Chase is still editor of his paper, and *The Bee* buzzes as of old.

THE FREEMAN FIRST ILLUSTRATED NEGRO WEEKLY

The first illustrated Negro newspaper was *The Indianapolis Freeman*, founded by Edward Cooper of Indianapolis, Ind., July 14, 1888. The paper consisted of eight pages, and gave a complete review of the doings of Negroes everywhere. The extensive use of cuts and illustrations made the paper famous. As an all around newspaperman, Cooper was without a peer, and under his management the paper reached a pre-eminent position in Negro Journalism. Today *The Freeman* is owned and controlled by George L. Knox, and it still enjoys a wide range of popularity. The paper features theatricals and sports. The present circulation is about 30,000.

AFRO-AMERICAN FOUNDED IN 1893

The founding of *The Afro-American* in 1893, by W. M. Alexander marks the beginning of a paper which today figures most conspicuously in Negro Journalism. About 1896, the paper came into the hands of J. H. Murphy, Sr., who is now its managing editor at the age of eighty. More will be said of *The Afro-American* in connection with the chapter on Present Day Papers.

LEADING PAPERS IN 1897

A list of the leading Negro newspapers in America in 1897, compiled by J. T. Haley in his book *Sparkling Gems of Race Knowledge*, includes the following: *The Colored American*, Washington, D. C.; *The New York Age*; *The Indianapolis Freeman*; *The Cleveland Gazette*; *The Boston Courant*; *The Richmond* (Va.) *Planet*; *The Huntsville* (Ala.) *Gazette*; *The Southern Age*, Atlanta, Ga.; *The Progress*, Helena, Ark.; *The Elevator*, San Francisco, Cal.; *The Colorado Statesman*, Denver, Colo.; *The Appeal*, Chicago, Ill.; *The Afro-American*, Baltimore, Md., and *The Denver* (Colo.) *Star*.

ORGANIZATION OF NEGRO CORRESPONDENTS

It would be improper to close a discussion of the period without mentioning the organizing of the "Associated Correspondents of Race Papers" on April 23, 1890. The object of the organization was to establish a better medium of communication from the capital. This step was perhaps the first real effort for unison among Negro newspapers, and marked a growing spirit of journalistic co-operation and interdependency.

[5]Murphy died in April, 1922, at the age of 80 years.

CHAPTER V

THE DAWN OF A NEW ERA (1900:–)

JOURNALISM BECOMING A PROFESSION

Without doubt the first two decades of the twentieth century mark the highest progress in Negro Journalism. More papers have been established, and better papers have been produced. A realization of the power of the press has grown as the period of freedom has increased and race consciousness has been developed. More men with capital have invested in newspapers. Publishers and editors began for the first time to consider Journalism a profession from which a living could be derived.

LACK FUNDS AND NEED EQUIPMENT

Lack of adequate funds to fully develop a well-balanced newspaper has been and still is the greatest drawback to the Negro publisher. Until in very recent years, no Negro newspaper did all of its mechanical work. In many cases the newspaper office merely collected and arranged the news, and then carried it to some publishing concern. In other cases, the paper was printed by a publishing house, although the "forms" were made-up in the paper's own shop. Thus, Negro newspapers have not been independent concerns.

LACK OF LIVE NEWS STORIES

In his effort to seriously make journalistic progress, the

publisher of a Negro newspaper has always found it difficult to obtain sufficient live material to fill up his sheet. There have been no news bureaus or syndicates to supply him with the type of news needed to make his paper a real newsy sheet. In his endeavor to "pad out" in order to continually fill the standard size of his paper, the Negro publisher has been compelled to "clip" news previously featured by the daily newspapers or rewrite news from other Negro papers—a task rendered difficult by the corresponding dearth of real news in all Negro papers during "dull" seasons.

POOR ORGANIZATION A SERIOUS HANDICAP

Prior to and at the beginning of the twentieth century, the organization of the average Negro newspaper amounted to a printer-editor, perhaps an assistant whose duties were varied and manifold, an office girl, who in addition to keeping books, also performed the duties of copy-reader, and two or three agents who worked part time on a percentage basis. The typographical and grammatical structure of many of the papers suffered greatly through the lack of having a staff sufficiently trained and equipped with the proper facilities for turning out a well-edited, well-printed sheet.

Dependence on a small, under-paid and inefficient organization—a condition analogous, and in many instances worse than that which exists on the small town newspaper—has seriously handicapped the Negro newspaper of the past.

NEWS BUREAUS AND SYNDICATES FOUNDED

The past twenty years have witnessed the evolution of a new Negro press. Stronger papers have been begun, and news syndicates and news associations have been founded. Examples of the latter are: The Hampton Institute Service, The Tuskegee

Institute Press Service, Allen's News Agency, The R. W. Thompson News Agency, The National Negro Press Association and The Associated Negro Press. Especially is the last named organization rendering a great service and filling a great need.

ASSOCIATED NEGRO PRESS

The Associated Negro Press has been in existence less than four years but during that time it has rapidly grown and achieved great success. Today it has a membership of more than 100 newspapers. The establishment of the A. N. P. was the first effort in Negro Journalism to assemble and distribute regularly general news from all sections of the United States and other countries affecting Colored people. Through the work of this organization big news stories now appear simultaneously in all of the leading Negro newspapers. The A. N. P. maintains executive offices in Chicago and permanent bureaus in Washington and New York.

PAPERS OF THE PERIOD

Among the present day papers established in this period are: *The Boston Guardian*, *The Nashville Globe*, *The Atlanta Independent*, *The Chicago Defender*, *The Detroit Leader*, *The Pittsburgh Courier*, *The St. Louis Argus*, *The Dallas Express*, *The Cleveland Advocate*, *The Negro World*, *The Indianapolis Ledger*, *The Indianapolis Recorder*, and *The Chicago Whip*.

GEORGE W. GORE

CHAPTER VI

PRESENT DAY PAPERS

250 Secular Weeklies

Today over 250 secular Negro newspapers are being published in the United States, with a total circulation of over one million five hundred thousand copies. These papers are published in 34 states and in the district of Columbia.

Papers Have Journalistic Appearance

Papers published in the larger centers where the Negro population is large, such as New York City, Chicago, Boston, Philadelphia, Cleveland, St. Louis, Washington, Detroit, Indianapolis, Baltimore, Pittsburgh, Nashville and Atlanta have developed to a high degree. Their make-up on the whole is good; their news stories for the most part conform with accepted journalistic style; their leads are of the summary type; their headlines, although somewhat sensational, are usually well constructed; their news treatment is becoming more impersonal; on the whole they are a great improvement over the Negro papers of the past.

Defender Housed in $200,000 Plant

Negro newspaper offices are being transformed from mere receiving stations for news to newspaper plants. During May, 1921, *The Chicago Defender*, one of the leading Negro newspapers, moved into a new building fitted up by its owner, Robert S. Abbott, at an expense of over $200,000. The new *Defender* plant compares favorably with that of any paper of its size in the United States. Its equipment includes four linotype machines, each equipped with two magazines, geared to cast seven lines per minute. The press on which *The Defender* is printed is a 32-page and color machine, made by the celebrated Goss Printing Press Company. It is driven by a 30 H.P. motor and six men are required for its operation. It prints, folds and counts the papers all in one operation at a speed of 35,000 copies per hour. The paper's circulation is over 200,000.

Abbott, Editor and Owner of The Chicago Defender, Chicago, Illinois

AFRO-AMERICAN EMPLOYS 21

Another paper which is representative of the new order of things in Negro Journalism is *The Afro-American* of Baltimore, Md. *The Afro-American* was among the first Negro papers to own and operate its own plant. Today the plant consists of a three-story building, Goss Press, three linotype machines, etc. The paper has twenty-one active employees and over two hundred agents in the state. The sworn circulation of the paper for 1920-21 was twenty thousand and one hundred copies weekly.

TRIBUNE OWNS $100,000 PLANT

From a humble beginning in 1884, *The Philadelphia Tribune* has grown until today it has its own hundred thousand dollar plant, fully equipped to do modern job and commercial work in addition to printing the paper. Christopher J. Perry remained sole owner of the paper from its founding to the time of his death. Today the paper is being published by his children, and is continuing along the conservative lines which have characterized the paper for more than 35 years.

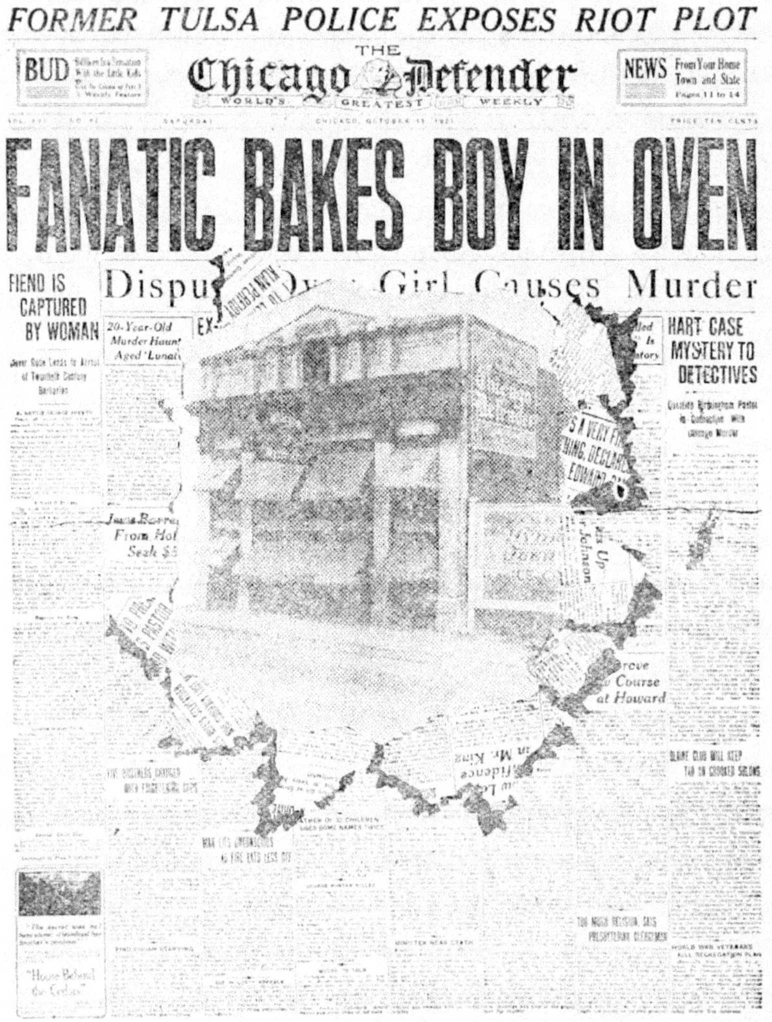

First page of the Chicago Defender, a leading Negro weekly newspaper with a $200,000 plant and a subscription list which is over 175,000. A view of the plant is also shown.

Better Staffs and News

In the past, the editorial page has been the one redeeming feature of the average Negro newspaper. Today the papers are beginning to have well-balanced staffs, reporters, city editors, cartoonists, etc. News stories are being better written, copy is being handled more carefully, accuracy is being insisted upon, and make-up in general is being improved.

Sectional Differences in Development

Papers printed in different parts of the country vary quite significantly in their make-up and quality. The best papers are probably published in the Middle West and the East. The Southern press is still in the rear, although signs are evident that it is beginning to wake up. At the present four Southern papers have a very high national rating. They are *The Afro-American*, *The Atlanta Independent*, *The Nashville Globe* and *The Dallas Express*.

Papers Having Over 30,000

Seven papers have over 30,000 subscribers. The list includes the following papers in the order named: *The Chicago Defender*, *The Negro World*, *The Indianapolis Ledger*, *The Atlanta Independent*, *The New York News*, *The Pittsburgh Courier* and *The Birmingham Reporter*.

Twelve Leading Negro Weeklies

Any attempt to select the leading Negro newspapers of necessity must be more or less arbitrary, and dependent upon prejudices toward certain types of journalism. A probable list of the best twelve weeklies might include: *The Chicago Defender*, *The Afro-American*, *The Cleveland Advocate*, *The Philadelphia Tribune*, *The New York Age*, *The Pittsburgh*

Courier, The Chicago Whip, The St. Louis Argus, The Indianapolis Ledger, The Atlanta Independent, The Detroit Leader and *The Boston Guardian.*

28

CHAPTER VII

DAILY NEGRO NEWSPAPERS

FIRST DAILY CAIRO GAZETTE

The first attempt of the Negro journalist to publish a daily newspaper was *The Cairo* (Ill.) *Gazette*, which was first issued April 23, 1882. The editor was W. S. Scott. The paper was issued regularly for six months when the plant was destroyed by fire. It was a readable sheet, contained much original matter, and had a good force of reporters.

COLUMBUS MESSENGER

The next attempt was *The Columbus Messenger*, published at Columbus. Ga. It was first issued as a daily in 1888. It was edited by B. T. Harvey, a graduate of Tuskegee Institute. The sheet was 12 by 20 inches.

DAILIES ISSUED FOR SHORT PERIODS

Several newspapers have issued daily editions for short periods. *The Knoxville* (Tenn.) *Negro World* was issued daily as an advertising medium for two weeks. About 1890 *The Public Ledger* of Baltimore, Md., was issued daily by Wesley Adams, for a short period. *The Nashville Globe* published a daily during the $30,000 Y. M. C. A. campaign in Nashville, Tenn., June 1-12, 1913. It proved a tremendous success for the twelve days and had an average circulation of 5,000 per day. During the World War *The Herald* of Baltimore, Md., edited by W. T. Andrews, was issued daily.

DAILIES IN FORM OF "BROADSIDES"

Three daily papers are being published at present. Two of these, *The Richmond* (Va.) *Colored American* and *The Washington Colored American* are published by the American Publicity Bureau, Inc. and The National Negro Publicity Bureau, Inc., respectively with D. Eugene Taylor listed as general manager of both. In form these papers are "broadsides"—a bulletin type of sheet printed on only one side. They are printed on a sheet measuring 24 inches by 36 inches. The news is set in two double columns, running down the center of the page between a double column of advertising on each side.

DAILY STANDARD

The third paper is *The Indianapolis Daily Standard* which began publication the latter part of April, 1922, under the editorship of C. C. Shelby. It is a 7 column, 4-page paper and retails at 2 cents per copy.

DRAWBACKS TO NEGRO DAILY

The slow development of the Negro daily is due chiefly to the fact: (1) That the field of such papers is already covered to a large extent by the American daily press; and (2) That a daily paper, with a restricted field from which to gather news, and denied the service of the Associated Press, is well nigh impossible. With the further development of the Associated Negro Press more Negro dailies may be possible.

CHAPTER VIII
NEGRO MAGAZINES

EARLY MAGAZINES

The magazine field has not been entered as rapidly or as fully by the Negro journalist as the newspaper field. The first Negro magazine, nevertheless, early followed the beginning made by the first Negro newspaper. In 1837, the first magazine—*The Mirror of Liberty*—was published by David Ruggles. It was devoted to the advancement of the free Negroes in the North, and was issued quarterly from New York City.

ANGLO-AFRICAN MAGAZINE

The next serious attempt to publish a Negro magazine was in 1856, when Thomas Hamilton, of New York City, issued *The Anglo-African Magazine*, which was the outgrowth of his newspaper, The Anglo-African. It was devoted to literature, science, statistics and contained articles on the abolition of slavery. It existed for about four years.

A. M. E. REVIEW OLDEST MAGAZINE

The oldest Negro magazine, like the oldest newspaper, was established by the A. M. E. Church. In 1884, that denomination began the publishing of *The A. M. E. Review* in Baltimore, Md. Today it still exists and is published in Philadelphia, Pa.

Our Women and Children

Another noteworthy periodical is *Our Women and Children*, first published in 1888, by Dr. William J. Simmons. It was unique in that it practically confined itself to the feminine world. Its contributors were chiefly women and the articles which appeared on its pages concerned themselves primarily with questions which affected home-life.

Over 100 Magazines in Existence

Many other Negro magazines have been attempted; many of more or less note, but of the magazines established prior to 1900, scarcely a one, if any, are in existence today. Of the leading present day magazines, none can boast of as long a period of publication as the present day newspapers. At present about one hundred magazines are being published by Negroes. However, this number includes school periodicals, church organs and fraternal organs, and only a small fraction of the total number are purely literary or secular publications.

The Crisis Edited by Dr. DuBois

Among the foremost Negro magazines of general literature is *The Crisis*, published at New York City, under the editorship of Dr. W. E. B. DuBois, perhaps the leading literary figure among the race today. While the publication is the official organ of the National Association for the Advancement of Colored People, it contains short stories, essays, sketches and poetry of a high literary quality.

Special Educational Number

A special feature of *The Crisis* is the emphasis it places on higher education. Each July it publishes an educational number containing the photographs of Negro college graduates from white Northern institutions during the past school year. The issue also contains a resume of the educational progress of the year.

The Messenger, a Journal of Social Science

The Messenger, published in New York City by Phillip Randolph and Chandler Owen, is devoted to economic, political and sociological subject-matter, with special emphasis upon the Negro and his relation to the labor problem. The tremendous influence of this magazine, devoted as it is to such a special field, is clearly shown by the fact that at present it has a circulation of over 26,000.

A Magazine Devoted to Music and Sports

Another magazine which confines itself to a limited field is *The American Musician and Sportsman Magazine*. This publication is printed in Philadelphia, Pa., by William A. Potter, editor. It is intended to afford opportunity for the expression of opinion on things musical, and in addition to its emphasis on music it deals with all branches of professional and amateur sports. The magazine has a circulation of 5500.

Journal of Negro History

One of the most scholarly periodicals published by Negroes is *The Journal of Negro History* edited by Carter G. Woodson, Ph.D., at Washington, D. C. The publication treats in a thorough-going and detailed manner the history of the Negro race.

Brownies' Book for Negro Youth

The Brownies' Book, a magazine devoted to the activities of the Negro youth, is also published in New York City and has at its head Dr. DuBois and Augustus Dill. It contains stories, the life and deeds of famous men and women of the Negro race, and current events of the world told in language suitable for children. In a similar manner to *The Crisis*, it features the photographs of Negro high school graduates.

FEATURED NEGRO SHORT STORIES

Two magazines of national importance and published in Chicago, Ill., are *The Half-Century*, edited by Katherine Williams Irmin and *The Favorite*, edited by Fenton Johnson. Both of these periodicals feature literary material and short stories dealing with Negro life.

THE RADIATOR

Another periodical dealing with a special field is *The Radiator*, a bi-monthly insurance magazine, edited by Sadie T. Mossell at Durham, N. C. Its purpose is to disseminate news and information to Negro insurance companies and workers.

LEADING PRESENT DAY MAGAZINES

Other magazines published at the present time are: *The Journal of the National Medical Association*, issued quarterly by the National Medical Association at Tuskegee Institute, Ala.; *The Pullman Porter's Review*, Chicago, Ill.; *The Search Light*, Raleigh, N. C.; *The Rainbow*, New York City, and *The Crusader*, New York City.

CHAPTER IX

TRAINING IN NEGRO SCHOOLS

ELEMENTARY TRAINING IN HIGH SCHOOLS

Definite steps are being taken by Negro schools and colleges to provide academic training in Journalism. Even in the high schools, the development of a vague appreciation of, and elementary training in Journalism is afforded by the publishing of school papers, under the supervision of the English department. Such schools as Dunbar High School, Washington, D. C.; Summer High School, St. Louis, Mo.; Central High School, Louisville, Ky.; Pearl High School, Nashville, Tenn., and Langston High School, Hot Springs, Ark., illustrate the point.

COLLEGE PUBLICATIONS

What is true of the high schools is true of the Normal and Industrial schools and colleges on a larger scale. Approximately one hundred periodicals are published by such institutions at least once a month. Some of these are purely the product of the student body; a few of them are the product of both students and faculty; still others are the publication of the administration and faculty, and under the supervision of a university editor. Many of the latter have developed to the place where they are nationally known. Such periodicals as *The Fisk University News*, *The Southern Workman* (Hampton Institute), *Howard University Record* (quarterly), *The Tuskegee Student* and *The Atlanta University Bulletin* (quarterly) are among the best Negro publications in the United States.

JOURNALISM COURSES AT FISK UNIVERSITY

This, however, is not all. The training of Negro journalists is being attempted through college courses. Fisk University, Nashville, Tenn., perhaps, was the first school to give such courses. Under the professorship of Isaac Fisher, one of the foremost Negro editors today, four courses in Journalism are offered. The course as outlined in the latest Fisk University catalog includes: (1) Essentials in Newspaper Technique—a course including practise in writing, editing, and methods of presentation; (2) The Law of Journalism—a study of libel, copyright, rights and duties of the press in reporting judicial proceedings, and the liabilities of the publisher, editor, reporter and contributor; (3) Ethics of Journalism—lectures discussing the proper responsibility to the public on the part of newspaper writers; (4) Art of Newspaper and Magazine Making—a course devoted to the studying of actual work of making a newspaper and magazine, with laboratory practice to supplement the theory studied.

PROFESSIONAL TRAINING

What will in all probabilities mark the real beginning of professional training in Journalism among Negroes is the opening of the proposed School of Journalism by Howard University, Washington, D. C. Owing to a limitation of finances, unfortunately the school has not yet been put in operation.

PROPOSED COURSES AT HOWARD UNIVERSITY JOURNALISM SCHOOL

The course as outlined in the Howard University catalog is based upon two years of college work, including a reading knowledge of at least two modern languages, and advanced work in English Composition. The professional work covers two years and leads to the degree of Bachelor of Science in Journalism. The subjects offered are: Practice in Writing, Newspaper Technique, Newspaper Editing, The History of Journalism, Advertising, Journalistic French, Journalistic German, Journalistic Spanish, Elements of Law, Freehand and Applied Drawing, and certain college courses in History, Economics, Sociology, Literature and Politics.

JOURNALISM AT WILBERFORCE

While it does not have a separate department in Journalism, Wilberforce University offers courses in journalistic writing as a part of the work in the department of English. Three courses are given at present: Business English, Short Story Writing and Editorial Writing.

PRINTING

On the mechanical side of newspaper publishing, work is offered in printing at Hampton Institute (Va.), Tuskegee Institute (Ala.), and Wilberforce University (Ohio). Many of the present printer-editors are products of these schools.

GEORGE W. GORE

CHAPTER X

A FORECAST OF THE FUTURE

From its small beginning in 1827, Negro Journalism has steadily grown in the United States. Today it stands as a definite factor in Negro life. In truth, the Negro press reflects the growing race consciousness of eleven million American citizens of African descent. The status of the Negro newspaper is fixed—it is here to stay. While daily newspapers may devote space to "News of Interest to Colored People;" yet they can never take the place of the newspapers which are published solely for the race group. The appeal of the Negro newspaper is direct and racial. In a manner similar to that of the rural press, the Negro paper has an unlimited field because of its personal relationship to its readers.

During the first half century of Negro Journalism, it is doubtful if any of the papers were financial successes; in truth, most of them were published as purely partisan or propagandists organs, and were supported through the contributions of sympathizers. Today Negro newspapers are conducted on business principles and pay reasonable returns to their investors.

Papers in the large cities have built up enormous subscription lists of bona fide, paid-up subscribers. Likewise, they carry a large amount of well-paying advertisements, and as a result of these sources of income they are able to give attractive remuneration to their publishers, editorial staff and business staff. No longer must the Negro journalist necessarily be an unpaid worker.

Trained journalists can obtain respectable salaries and find as many openings as their fellow workers on metropolitan dailies and national weeklies and monthlies.

That the calibre of the work done on Negro publications will continue to improve is highly probable in view of the fact that every year an increasing number of trained young men and women are entering the field, and bringing with them burning enthusiasm and high professional ideals. The Courses in Journalism in the Negro colleges, also, will soon be having a telling effect on the future Negro journalist. Already a few of the twentieth century Negro youths are being attracted to the professional study of Journalism, preferring the possibilities of its virgin field to the overcrowded professions of law, teaching, medicine and theology.

The future of Negro Journalism is limited only by the zeal and conscientious effort which its workers bestir themselves to exert. A marvelous growth and success has been recorded within the past 95 years, but greater achievement is yet to be accomplished. Negro semi-weeklies, and eventually dailies in the larger cities, will undoubtedly be developed within the next decade. The size of many of the present weeklies will be increased of necessity. Better news stories and more real news will be the result of the successful functioning of such news syndicates as the Associated Negro Press.

The decreasing of illiteracy among the Negroes will continue to be carried forward by the Negro press, with a mutual benefit to the race and its publications. Higher standards of literacy will bring greater appreciation for reading and thereby create a stronger support for the Negro publisher.

In the immediate future, perhaps, the great field for development in Negro Journalism is in the South where the great mass of Negro population, despite the Northern immigration, resides. There Negro Journalism needs and will continue to need its best trained editors and managers. There it will need men of sound judgment and common sense; men of purpose and high professional ideals; men of broad sympathy and great patience.

PARTIAL LIST OF NEWSPAPERS PUBLISHED IN THE UNITED STATES

ALABAMA

The Birmingham Reporter	Birmingham
The Emancipator	Montgomery
The Mobile Forum	Mobile
The Mobile Advocate	Mobile
The Mobile Weekly Press	Mobile
The Negro Leader	Uniontown
The Times Plaindealer	Birmingham
The Voice of the People	Birmingham
The Voice of the Negro	Dothan

ARKANSAS

Hot Springs Echo	Hot Springs
Arkansas Banner	Little Rock
The Appreciator-Union	Fort Smith
The Negro Advocate	Fordyce
The Interstate Reporter	Helena
The Opinion-Enterprise	Marianna
Western Review	Little Rock
White River Advocate	Newport

The School Herald	Warren

ARIZONA

The Phoenix Tribune	Phoenix

CALIFORNIA

The Eagle	Los Angeles
The Liberator	Los Angeles
The Citizens Advocate	Los Angeles
Oakland Sunshine	Oakland
The Western Outlook	Oakland
The New Age	Los Angeles
The Western Review	Sacramento

COLORADO

Colorado Statesman	Denver
The Denver Advocate	Colorado Springs
The Rising Sun	Pueblo

CONNECTICUT

Hartford Herald	Hartford

DISTRICT OF COLUMBIA

The Washington Eagle	Washington
The Washington Bee	Washington

FLORIDA

Florida Sentinel	Jacksonville
Labor Templar	Jacksonville
West Florida Bugle	Marianna
The Tampa Bulletin	Tampa
Metropolitan	Tallahassee

The Palatka Advocate	Palatka
The Colored Citizen	Pensacola

GEORGIA

The Savannah Journal	Savannah
The Savannah Tribune	Savannah
The Americus Chronicle	Americus
The Athens Clipper	Athens
The Atlanta Post	Atlanta
The Atlanta Independent	Atlanta
Rome Enterprise	Rome
The Advocate	Brunswick
The Augusta News	Augusta
Supreme Circle News	Albany

ILLINOIS

Inter-State Echo	Danville
The Broad Axe	Chicago
The Chicago Defender	Chicago
The Chicago Idea	Chicago
The Peoples Advocate	Chicago
The Searchlight	Chicago
The Whip	Chicago
The Forum	Springfield
The Weekly Star	Mound City
The Illinois Conservator	Springfield
Advance Citizens	Springfield

INDIANA

The Indianapolis Freeman	Indianapolis
The Indianapolis Recorder	Indianapolis
The Indianapolis Ledger	Indianapolis
The Indianapolis World	Indianapolis
The Terre Haute Citizen	Terre Haute
National Defender and Sun	Gary
The Gary Dispatch	Gary

IOWA

Iowa State Bystander	Des Moines
Buxton Gazette	Buxton

KANSAS

The Topeka Plaindealer	Topeka
The Negro Star	Wichita
Wichita Protest	Wichita
The Coffeyville Globe	Coffeyville
Hutchinson Blade	Hutchinson

KENTUCKY

The Kentucky Reporter	Louisville
The Columbian Herald	Louisville
The Louisville News	Louisville
Kentucky Home Finder	Louisville
Lexington Weekly News	Lexington
The Torchlight	Danville
Saturday News	Hopkinsville

| The New Age | Hopkinsville |

LOUISIANA

The Advance Messenger	Alexandria
The News-Enterprise	Shreveport
The Watchman	Shreveport

MARYLAND

The Afro-American	Baltimore
The Crusader	Baltimore
The Herald-Commonwealth	Baltimore

MASSACHUSETTS

| The Guardian | Boston |
| The Boston Chronicle | Boston |

MICHIGAN

| The Michigan Age | Ann Arbor |
| The Detroit Leader | Detroit |

MINNESOTA

| The National Advocate | Minneapolis |
| The Appeal | St. Paul |

MISSISSIPPI

The Cotton Farmer	Scott
The Delta Lighthouse	Greenville
The Natchez Weekly Herald	Natchez
The National Star	Vicksburg
The Star	Columbus
The Morning Star	Columbus
The Mississippi Monitor	Meridan

The Light	Vicksburg
The New Era	Indianola
The Weekly Times	Hattiesburg
The Weekly Reporter	Natchez
Central Mississippi Signal	Kosciusko
The Progressive Torchlight	Greenwood
The Advance	Mound Bayou
The National Defender	Clarksdale
The Informer	Gulfport
The National News Digest	Mound Bayou

MISSOURI

The St. Louis Independent-Clarion	St. Louis
The St. Louis Argus	St. Louis
The Anchor	Caruthersville
The Missouri State Register	Hannibal
Kansas City Sun	Kansas City
The National Mirror	Kansas City
The Western Messenger	Jefferson City
The St. Louis Independent News	St. Louis

NEBRASKA

The Monitor	Omaha

NEW JERSEY

The Eastern Observer	Montclair
The Echo	Red Bank
The Atlantic Advocate	Atlantic City

The New Jersey Informer	Newark

NEW YORK

The New York News	New York City
The Amsterdam News	New York City
The New York Age	New York City
The Negro World	New York City
The Commoner	New York City

NORTH CAROLINA

The Gate City Argus	Greensboro
High Point Colored American	High Point
The Charlotte Advertiser	Charlotte
The Voice	Rocky Mount
The Raleigh Independent	Raleigh
The Home News	Wilmington
The Gazette	Charlotte
Signs of the Times	Elizabeth City
The Winston-Salem News	Winston-Salem

OHIO

The Dayton Forum	Dayton
The Cleveland Gazette	Cleveland
The Cleveland Advocate	Cleveland
The Union	Cincinnati
The Cincinnati Journal	Cincinnati

OKLAHOMA

The Boley Progress	Boley
The Oklahoma Guide	Guthrie

The Muskogee Scimetar	Muskogee
Rentiesville News	Rentiesville
Clearview Patriarch	Clearview
The Tulsa Star	Tulsa
The Oklahoma Sun	Tulsa
The Black Dispatch	Oklahoma City

OREGON

| The Advocate | Portland |

PENNSYLVANIA

The Advocate Verdict	Harrisburgh
The Philadelphia Courant	Philadelphia
The Philadelphia Tribune	Philadelphia
The Philadelphia American	Philadelphia
The Public Journal	Philadelphia
The Pittsburgh Courier	Pittsburgh
The Pittsburgh American	Pittsburgh
The Advocate	Wilkes-Barre

RHODE ISLAND

| The Advance | Providence |

SOUTH CAROLINA

The Charleston Messenger	Charleston
The New Era	Charleston
The Allendale Advocate	Allendale
The Southern Indicator	Columbia
The Informer	Columbia
The Light	Columbia

The Plowman	Columbia
The Negro Chronicle	Greenville
The People's Recorder	Orangeburg
The Rockhill Messenger	Rockhill

TENNESSEE

Bluff City News	Memphis
East Tennessee News	Knoxville
Chattanooga Defender	Chattanooga
Memphis Times	Memphis
The Western World Reporter	Memphis
The Nashville Globe	Nashville
The Nashville Clarion	Nashville

TEXAS

Texas Guide	Victoria
The Victoria Guard	Victoria
The Calvert Bugle	Calvert
The City Times	Galveston
The Galveston New Idea	Galveston
The Dallas Express	Dallas
The Industrial Era	Beaumont
The Herald	Austin
The Watchman	Austin
The Houston Informer	Houston
The Houston Observer	Houston
The Texas Freeman	Houston
The Western Star	Houston
The Houston Informer	Houston

Independence Heights Record	Houston
The San Antonio Inquirer	San Antonio
The Gem City Bulletin	Denison
The Conservative Counselor	Waco
Fort Worth Hornet	Fort Worth

VIRGINIA

The Charlottesville Messenger	Charlottesville
The Colored Virginian	Petersburg
The Weekly Review	Petersburg
The Richmond Planet	Richmond
The Virginia Headlight	Charlottesville
The Virginia Advocate	Roanoke
The Star	Newport News
The Journal and Guide	Norfolk

WASHINGTON

The Seattle Searchlight	Seattle

WEST VIRGINIA

The Advocate	Charleston
The Mountain Leader	Charleston
The Charleston Observer	Charleston
The Pioneer Press	Martinsburg

WISCONSIN

The Wisconsin Weekly Blade	Madison

TRADE LINOTYPE MARK

Every important improvement in methods of composition for the past 36 years has been the result of LINOTYPE initiative.

Every part of the LINOTYPE is there because the machine is better for it and every part fits into the big scheme of simple operation. The LINOTYPE is the machine of no compromise.

54

LINOTYPE

® TRADE MARK ®

55

Every important improvement in methods of composition for the past 36 years has been the result of Linotype initiative.

Every part of the Linotype is there because the machine is better for it and every part fits into the big scheme of simple operation. The Linotype is the machine of no compromise.

The illustration shows the Model 21, text and display Linotype. As many as ten faces in six different sizes are immediately available from the keyboard.

This advertisement composed entirely on the LINOTYPE

We represent at the present time in the advertising field, practically every paper of consequence reaching the Colored people of the United States.

We are pleased to extend our most cordial greetings to our newspaper friends and will continue to extend the same reliable service in the future, we have given in the past.

W. B. ZIFF CO.
Per E. C. Auld, General Mgr.

Transportation Bldg., Chicago, Ill.	Morton Bldg. New York, N. Y.	Bryant Bldg. Kansas City, Mo.

DEPAUW UNIVERSITY

Greencastle, Indiana

OFFERS COURSES IN—

* Introduction to Writing

* News Writing

* News Editing

* Editorial Writing

* Feature Writing

* Advertising Writing

* History of American Journalism

* Country Weekly

* Also Business English

Write for Bulletin
DIRECTOR
COURSE IN JOURNALISM

HOWARD UNIVERSITY
WASHINGTON, D. C.

* Founded by GENERAL O. O. HOWARD

* J. STANLEY DURKEE, A. M., Ph. D., D. D., President

* EMMETT J. SCOTT, A. M., LL. D., Secretary-Treasurer

COLLEGIATE AND PROFESSIONAL SCHOOLS

Junior College, covering the Freshman and Sophomore years and leading to the Senior Schools.

Senior Schools, consisting of the Schools of Liberal Arts, Education, Journalism, and Commerce and Finance, granting respectively the degrees, A. B., or B. S., A. B. or B. S. in Education; B. S. in Journalism; B. S. in Commerce and Finance.

School of Applied Science, four year course, granting the degree, B. S. in Civil Engineering, B. S. in Electrical Engineering, B. S. in Mechanical Engineering, B. S. in Architecture, B. S. in Agriculture, and B. S. in Household Economics.

Evening Classes. The work of the Junior College and the Senior Schools may be taken in evening classes with full credit.

School of Music, four year course, granting the degree of Mus. B.

School of Religion, three year course, granting the degrees of B. D. and Th. B. Courses are offered also by correspondence.

School of Law, three year course, granting the degree of LL. B.

School of Medicine, including Medical, Dental, Pharmaceutical Colleges. Four year courses for Medical and Dental students; three year course for Pharmaceutical students. Following degrees granted: M. D., D. D. S., Phar. C.

58

STUDENTS MAY ENTER FOR COLLEGIATE WORK

AT THE BEGINNING OF ANY QUARTER.

REGISTRATION

Autumn Quarter	Sept. 29, 30, 1922
Winter Quarter	Jan. 2, 1923
Spring Quarter	March 17, 1923

FOR CATALOG AND INFORMATION WRITE

F. D. WILKINSON, Registrar

HOWARD UNIVERSITY WASHINGTON, D. C.